KU-274-899

**LEARN ABOUT DIFFERENT FAMILIES ON PAGE 56**

Quarto is the authority on a wide range of topics.
Quarto educates, entertains and enriches the lives of
our readers—enthusiasts and lovers of hands-on living.
www.quartoknows.com

Author: Lizzie Cox
Illustrator: Damien Weighill
Consultant: John Rees
Editor: Alice Bowden
Designer: Tracy Killick
QED Editor: Carly Madden
QED Designer: Victoria Kimonidou

Copyright © QED Publishing 2017

First published in the UK in 2017 by
QED Publishing
Part of The Quarto Group
The Old Brewery, 6 Blundell Street,
London, N7 9BH

A catalogue record for this book is available from
the British Library.

ISBN 978 1 78493 830 7

Printed in China

**MIX**
Paper from
responsible sources
FSC® C101537
FSC
www.fsc.org

# SO WHAT IS PUBERTY?

You've probably heard people talking about 'going through puberty', but what on earth does that 'P' word mean? **PUBERTY** is the name for all the changes your body goes through as you grow from a girl into a woman. Yes, you do have to be a grown-up one day. **YUCK.** (Only joking, mum).

You've been growing ever since you were born (obviously, otherwise you'd still be rolling around on the floor in a nappy), but puberty is when the biggest changes happen to your body, both physically **AND** emotionally.

## When does it start?

The important thing to remember is that there's no set or 'normal' time for puberty to begin. So you can put that calendar away – circling a date and writing 'PUBERTY STARTS' won't work here. Sorry!

Changes like: developing breasts, starting your period, growing hair in places where there **DEFINITELY** wasn't hair before, and feeling feelings that are totally new to you.

## All aboard!

All sounds like quite a lot to deal with, doesn't it? Well, HAVE NO FEAR – by the end of this book, you'll be clued up about what's going to happen, and fully prepared for the puberty train.

THIS IS NO FUN. I WANT TO GET OFF!

## The beginning

Most girls usually begin puberty anywhere between the ages of 8 and 14, but some will start seeing changes earlier, and some later – puberty is different for everyone.

The rate at which all these changes happen also differs from person to person. Some might go through puberty in a year or less, while others take up to seven years to finish developing fully.

When it comes to puberty there is no right or wrong: it happens when it happens, and it takes as long as it takes. What we're trying to say is **DON'T PANIC** or worry about developing before or after your friends – it all evens out in the end.

# BUT... WHAT MAKES PUBERTY HAPPEN?

Are you ready for **THE SCIENCE BIT?** *dramatic music*. It's all about hormones. Hormones are chemicals in your body that travel around in the blood telling your cells and organs to do certain things. Think of them as little chemical messengers that kickstart puberty, then carry on telling your body how to develop and change as you become an adult.

WOO-HOO!

YAY, PARTY!

**STAGE 1** It all starts when one of those hormones we talked about travels to a pea-sized place at the base of your brain, called the pituitary gland. The hormone arrives and tells the gland to release new, different hormones, which it does. Your body is now a **HORMONE PARTY.**

**STAGE 2** Now that all those hormones are racing around your body, the more noticeable physical changes begin. You may notice what feel like little buttons beneath your nipples. This is a sign that your breasts are beginning to develop (**see p.10–11**). You'll also get taller, and start growing pubic hair (the hair around your vulva) and hair under your arms.

**STAGE 3** Oh, it's all kicking off now! Your breasts will carry on growing, and your pubic hair will get thicker. Your hips will also get wider – this is to get your body ready for having a baby when you are grown up (if you want one!). Some girls also start to produce a clear or whitish discharge from their vagina, which is the totally normal way that your vagina cleans itself, the clever thing. This usually happens not long before your periods start.

I AM HERE TO DELIVER YOUR EGGS!

**STAGE 4** As you continue the puberty journey, you will become fertile. **'FERTILE'** is another way of saying **'ABLE TO HAVE A BABY'**, and means your ovaries will start releasing eggs into your womb, causing your periods to start. Your breasts will also continue to grow, and your nipples may get darker.

**STAGE 5** So how does puberty end? Well, you'll reach your full adult height, your breasts will finish developing, and your periods will start to follow a regular pattern, around once a month. Physically, you are now a woman. **PHEW!**

## Puberty checklist

- ☐ Feeling moody
- ☐ Getting taller
- ☐ Breasts start developing
- ☐ Growing pubic hair
- ☐ First period!

# THE BRAIN GAME

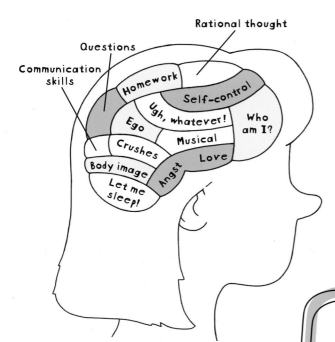

Rational thought
Questions
Communication skills
Homework
Self-control
Ego
Ugh, whatever!
Who am I?
Crushes
Musical
Body image
Love
Angst
Let me sleep!

It's not just your outside that changes when you hit puberty – your insides are changing too, including your brain.

The biggest development happens in the front area of your brain, called the **FRONTAL LOBE**. The frontal lobe is a bit of a bossy boots and basically tells the rest of your brain what to do. It isn't fully developed until you've finished puberty.

This means that as you start the physical changes – getting taller, growing breasts, starting your periods, and so on – you'll also become more **GROWN-UP** emotionally as your brain develops. It is being reshaped to become more efficient, like someone pruning a tree to make it grow better. But while the pruning is happening, you might feel like your emotions keep getting the better of you.

## Manage your moods

Take a break. Feel upset or angry? Find a quiet spot, take some deep breaths, and concentrate on something that makes you happy.

Snooze. When going through puberty you need a lot of sleep, so you don't get grouchy. Try and get at least 8 hours sleep a night.

Apologise. Everyone says things they don't mean sometimes, it's life – but an apology can make everything feel better.

# What's going on in my <u>brain</u>?

Different areas of your brain start to connect more, and at the same time new brain connections are being made.

Brain pathways that you use a lot (like working out how to reach level two of your favourite computer game) start speeding up.

Old brain pathways that you hardly ever use (like playing with Lego) close down.

Your emotions work faster than the bit of the brain that keeps them in check, so they can feel a bit out of control sometimes.

## Getting emotional

What do you get when you take all of those new hormones having a party in your bloodstream, and combine them with your growing brain? A load of brand new emotions and feelings, that's what.

Puberty can be overwhelming, and you might find yourself having stronger and more extreme emotions. These are sometimes called **'MOOD SWINGS'**, because you may feel fine one minute, and then really sad or angry the next.

THIS IS A TRICKY BALANCING ACT!

It's important to know that this is **N.O.R.M.A.L.** You're in between being a child and a woman, and that's a lot to deal with. It's not surprising you might sometimes cry for no reason, or suddenly feel irritable and moody.

# LET'S TALK <u>BOOBS</u>

**BREASTS. BOOBS. MELONS.** They have many different names, but women have breasts for only one reason – to feed a baby. Breasts are made up of body tissue, ducts and glands. When a woman becomes pregnant, these glands start producing milk, ready for a mother to give her baby the best possible food when it's born.

Most girls begin developing breasts between the ages of 8 and 14. First your nipples will start growing and might become puffy or sore. These are known as '<u>breast buds</u>'. They'll then continue to grow for about five or six years (yep, **YEARS**), until they are fully developed.

DELICIOUS – NOW WHAT'S FOR DESSERT?

## REMEMBER

Breasts come in ALL KINDS of different shapes and sizes: there is no 'normal' or 'better' or 'right'.

## All boobs are normal

Boobs are one of the most obvious changes that happen during puberty, a change that everyone can see. This makes it easier to compare your breasts with others, and easier to worry that yours are too big or too small.

Some girls have small boobs, some have big boobs and others have something in between – we're all different and that's a good thing. Say it with us: **A. GOOD. THING**.

NORMAL

NORMAL

NORMAL

GUESS WHAT? THESE ARE NORMAL TOO!

## I have a question!

 My left boob looks different to my right boob, am I weird?

No, of course not! One side of your body is never a mirror image of the other, so it's entirely normal for one breast to be bigger/smaller or higher/lower than the other.

TOTALLY UPLIFTING

 My friends are all growing boobs so why am I still flat-chested?

It can be hard when you're the last to begin developing breasts, and just as tough if you're the first. Puberty is different for everybody, but you'll all get there eventually, when the time is right for you. **Hang in there!**

 My boobs feel lumpy, should I be worried?

As breasts grow they can often feel lumpy and sore, especially before a period. If, however, you notice a change or a lump that's been there for a few weeks, it's always best to talk to a doctor, just in case.

# BRA-MAZING: <u>EVERYTHING</u> YOU NEED TO KNOW

A bra is a piece of underwear used to support your breasts, with two cups (not the drinking kind), a back band and shoulder straps. Simple, right?

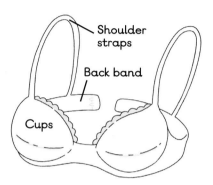

- Shoulder straps
- Back band
- Cups

## My first bra

It's up to you to decide when you want your first bra, there's no rule saying when this should happen. When the time feels right, have a chat with your mum, aunt, big sister, dad, **CAT\*** – whoever you're comfortable talking to.

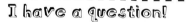

### I have a question!

I'm embarrassed for people to see my bra in the school changing rooms. Help!

Growing breasts is a natural part of becoming a woman so remember that everyone is going through exactly the same thing as you are.

I'm quite flat-chested but I want to wear a bra. Can I?

Of course you can. It's your body, your rules, your decision – your breasts don't have to be a certain size before you start wearing a bra. Just make sure it fits you properly.

My mum says I don't need a bra yet but I really want one, what can I do?

Sit her down and explain that this is something you really want, and ask what her reasons are. If you understand her point of view, and she understands yours, you might be able to reach a compromise.

\* YOUR CAT PROBABLY WON'T ACTUALLY BE ABLE TO HELP MUCH. JUST SAYING. \*

Training bra

## Which bra is best?

Most girls find that a **TRAINING BRA** is the best option to begin with. These are made of soft, stretchy material that gives your breasts room to grow.

When your boobs are more developed, there's a whole load of bra options, including many with underwire for extra support. <u>Try a couple of styles</u> to see which you find most comfortable.

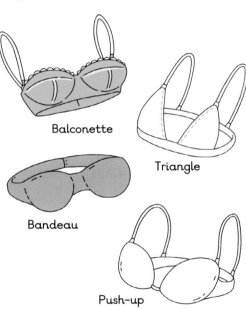

Balconette

Triangle

Bandeau

Push-up

## Bra-size checklist

☐ Does the back-band sit flat under your shoulder blades, without riding up?

☐ Do your breasts sit comfortably in the cups, without overflowing?

☐ Do the cups sit right against your skin, without any bagginess?

☐ Does the front of your bra sit flat against your chest without a gap?

If you didn't tick all of these boxes, you could be wearing the wrong bra size. Lots of underwear shops have a bra measuring service, so go and get measured rather than guessing.

Wearing a bra that fits correctly is **SO** important – if it's too big or too small it won't support your breasts properly, and can even cause back or shoulder pain. **OUCH!**

# PERIODS

Most girls get their first period between the ages of 10 and 14. However, it's also normal to start a year or two earlier or later, so don't worry if you wake up on your 14th birthday and you haven't had a period yet.

The scientific word for a period is 'menstruation'. A period is blood from your womb (uterus) leaving your body through your vagina. Don't worry, it's really not that scary. Sit back, relax and we'll explain **EVERYTHING**.

## PMT checklist

☐ Mood swings: feeling more grumpy or emotional than usual.

☐ Feeling extra tired and sleepy.

☐ Tender or swollen breasts.

☐ Feeling bloated.

☐ Cramp-like pains in your lower tummy and back.

It's fun being a girl, right?!

## Cramps, moods & more

Periods affect girls in different ways, but most will experience some form of **PMT** (which stands for Pre-Menstrual Tension) in the days before each period.

POOR BOYS, MISSING OUT ON ALL THIS JOY...

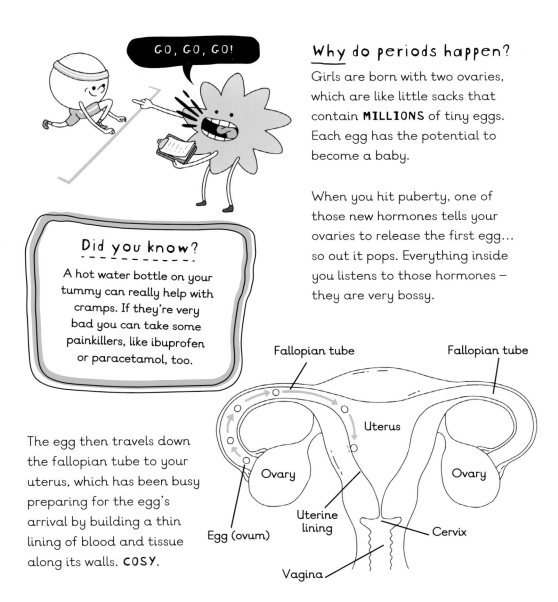

GO, GO, GO!

## Why do periods happen?

Girls are born with two ovaries, which are like little sacks that contain **MILLIONS** of tiny eggs. Each egg has the potential to become a baby.

When you hit puberty, one of those new hormones tells your ovaries to release the first egg… so out it pops. Everything inside you listens to those hormones – they are very bossy.

### Did you know?
- - - - - - - - - -
A hot water bottle on your tummy can really help with cramps. If they're very bad you can take some painkillers, like ibuprofen or paracetamol, too.

The egg then travels down the fallopian tube to your uterus, which has been busy preparing for the egg's arrival by building a thin lining of blood and tissue along its walls. **COSY.**

Fallopian tube

Fallopian tube

Uterus

Ovary

Ovary

Uterine lining

Cervix

Egg (ovum)

Vagina

If the egg isn't fertilized by a sperm before it enters the uterus (**see p.36**) then your body realises it's not pregnant and the lining breaks down, leaving your body as a period. **THAT'S WHAT THE BLOOD IS!** The blood can look thick or thin, clumpy or stringy, and be bright red or dark brown – this is all normal.

# Four things you need to know

**1.** It can take a while for your body to settle into a regular monthly cycle – so don't panic if you get your first period and then don't have another for a few months.

**2.** When your periods do become regular, you'll have one roughly every 28 days, and each period will last between 3 and 5 days (that's the time of actual bleeding).

**3.** You lose around one egg-cup full of blood each period. It may seem like LOADS more than that when you see it on your pad or tampon, but it's not!

**4.** A lot of girls notice a white, sticky substance in their underwear called 'discharge' in the months before their period. This is nothing to be worried about – it's just your body getting ready.

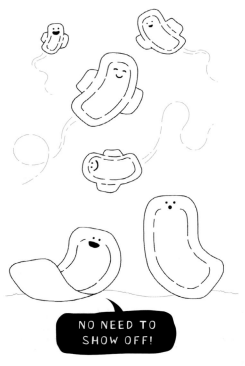

NO NEED TO SHOW OFF!

## What should **I** use?

When you start your period, you need something to soak up the blood. Let's take a look at your **OPTIONS**, shall we?

## Sanitary towels

In the beginning you'll probably feel most comfortable using sanitary towels – absorbent pads that stick to your underwear. There are two different types: with or without 'wings'. The wings help keep the pad securely in place for when you are more active. They need to be changed every few hours in the day. At night you can wear a thicker pad, so that you don't have to disturb your precious beauty sleep to change it!

## Tampons

A tampon sits <u>inside</u> the vagina and absorbs the blood. It is removed by gently pulling the string (which will **NOT** break off, **DON'T WORRY!**). Once you have learnt how to insert them properly, you can even swim with one in – it's perfectly safe and snug up there.

Most girls wait until they've had a few periods before using tampons, but this doesn't mean you can't use them right away if you feel comfortable.

### Toxic Shock Syndrome

It's VERY important to change your tampon every four to six hours, and it should never EVER be left in for longer than 9 hours. In very rare cases, tampons left in for too long can cause a nasty infection called Toxic Shock Syndrome (TSS) that will need to be treated in hospital.

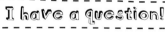

I have a question!

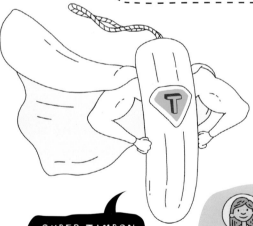

SUPER TAMPON READY FOR ACTION!

Can a tampon get lost inside of me?
**NO, NOPE AND NEVER.** At the top of your vagina is your cervix, and this only has a teeny tiny hole that's impossible for a tampon to get through. Phew!

I'm really scared my period will start at school – what should I do if it does?
The school nurse should have a sanitary towel or in an emergency you can put a wad of toilet paper in your underwear! If you're really worried, keep a spare pair of knickers and a sanitary towel in your school bag, just in case!

# HAIR WE GO

When puberty hits, so does hair growth. In fact, it can seem like it's popping up and getting thicker **EVERYWHERE** – from your face to your underarms, legs and around your vagina.

Age 9

Age 12

Age 15

### Did you know?

Body hair is actually really important and has loads of different uses, like keeping you warm, protecting your skin from germs or bacteria, and creating a barrier to reduce friction between you and your clothes.

The hair around your vagina is known as 'pubic' hair because it sits on the pubic bone... **CLEVER**. It's also usually more coarse, curly and wiry than the hair on your head, and will eventually form a rough triangle shape between your legs.

## Hair removal: what, when and why?

When they get older, some girls <u>choose</u> to remove body hair, while others don't. No one option is better, it's your – and only your! – choice. Remember this please: nobody should ever feel pressured by anyone else into changing his or her body, and that includes hair removal.

## Shaving

For your underarms and legs. Just be careful! Always use shaving foam, and change your razor before it gets all rusty as this can cause infection. **EEK!**

THAT WAS A CLOSE SHAVE!

## Hair removal cream

A cream containing chemicals that dissolve hair at the follicle on the skin's surface. Always read the instructions carefully, as leaving it on for too long can cause irritation.

TA-DAH! JUST LIKE MAGIC!

## Epilation

Epilation pulls your hairs out at the roots using an electronic device called an epilator. It can be used for legs and underarms, but only some are safe to use on the pubic area and face, so do check first.

## Tweezing or plucking

Hey, eyebrows, it's your turn. Tweezers pluck out individual hairs one by one. **GO SLOWLY** and keep standing back to check your work in the mirror. It's easy to get carried away!

OOOWWWWWW!

## Waxing

Can be used **ANYWHERE**, including more sensitive areas like your face or pubic area. Warm wax is applied then pulled off in a strip, ripping the hairs out at the roots. And yep – it can be quite painful!

# SPOTS & SKIN

While all those puberty hormones are having a party, they are also making your skin produce more oil, which clogs up your **PORES** (these are tiny little holes in your skin – look reeeeally closely and you'll see them). This can cause spots on your face, neck, shoulders and back. In more extreme cases, this can also lead to acne.

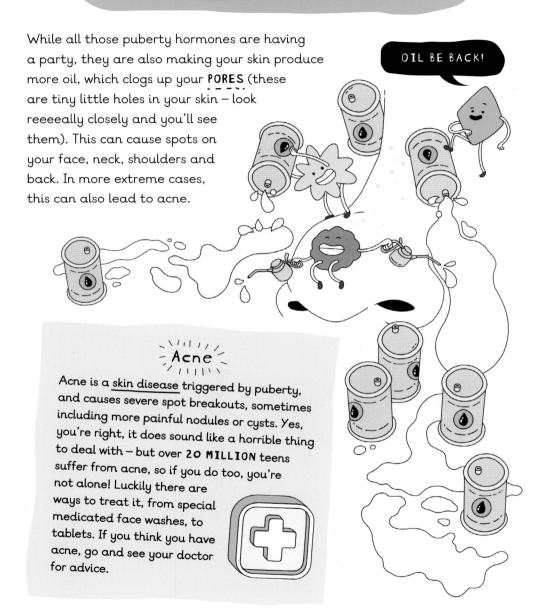

OIL BE BACK!

## Acne

Acne is a skin disease triggered by puberty, and causes severe spot breakouts, sometimes including more painful nodules or cysts. Yes, you're right, it does sound like a horrible thing to deal with – but over **20 MILLION** teens suffer from acne, so if you do too, you're not alone! Luckily there are ways to treat it, from special medicated face washes, to tablets. If you think you have acne, go and see your doctor for advice.

# Spot the difference

Unlike human beings, not all spots are created equal: there are different types. Here's how to **SPOT** (**HA HA!**) each kind, and how to deal with it.

## Whiteheads

The clue is in the name! These are small spots with whitish yellow 'heads' filled with pus, **YUCK**. They can be (gently) squeezed, but wash your hands first, or squeeze between a piece of clean tissue. If you have germs on your fingers, you'll just create more spots.

## Blackheads

See any tiny black or brown pin pricks? These are blackheads. They're blocked pores that are 'open'. The black colour is created when the bacteria inside reacts with the air around you. You can damage your skin if you try to squeeze these – use a face wash to get rid of them.

## Papules

These suckers are red, painful spots under the skin, created when trapped oil and bacteria have caused inflammation. They should definitely **NOT** be squeezed – just keep them clean and apply some spot cream.

# Give your skin some TLC

Because your skin is extra prone to spots when you hit puberty, you **NEED NEED NEED** to make sure you're cleaning it properly, and giving it some **TLC** (that's tender loving care, **DUH**).

**1.** Wash your face with a **GENTLE CLEANSER** in the morning <u>AND</u> at night, making sure not to scrub too hard (this can hurt your skin and make it sore).

**2.** Moisturise, moisturise, **MOISTURIIIIIIIISE.** You might think that all that skin oil means you don't need more moisture, but you do! If your skin gets too dry, it will react by producing even **MORE** oil, and this can lead to more spots.

**3.** You can then apply some **MEDICATED CREAM** from the chemist to any spots. Just make sure it's not too strong: you don't want to damage or irritate your skin. You can always ask someone who works in the chemist which product is best for you.

Wash your towels and pillowcases every two weeks, to get rid of GERMS.

Try not to touch your face with dirty fingers.

If you wear make-up, use oil-free products designed to be kind to skin. Ask an adult or someone in the shop if you're not sure which these are.

Always – yes, that's A_L_W_A_Y_S – take make-up off before bed!

SUPER SMOOTH...

...ALL OVER!

## Exfoliate!

It's not just your face that needs attention! Look after the skin on your body by using a gentle exfoliator when you shower. This is a type of body wash with little scrubbing particles in it that remove dead skin cells and dirt from your skin's surface. It helps to reduce spots that can pop up on your back and shoulders during puberty.

### Did you know?

If you wash your glasses (or sunglasses) regularly, it will help to stop spot-making grease building up.

# FACE IT: EYES & TEETH

As you grow, you need to make sure you're taking care of all your body's bits and bobs, from the top of your head to the tips of your toes. This includes your eyes and teeth – keep those peepers and gnashers in tip top condition.

## Glasses

Lots of people need glasses to help them see. If you find yourself squinting, or things look a little blurry, talk to an adult about going for an **EYE TEST**.

An optician will check out your eyesight using some <u>fun tests</u> involving lights, mirrors and lenses (don't worry, none are painful!). They can then tell you if you need glasses.

> I LOVE MY GLASSES. I LOOK COOL AND CLEVER!

## REMEMBER

You might feel a bit strange or embarrassed wearing glasses at first, but you shouldn't be. Glasses are cool – just ask Harry Potter! **WINGARDIUM LEVIOSA.**

## Contact lenses

Contacts are little curved lenses that you place on your eyeball and are pretty much **INVISIBLE**. They need cleaning carefully to avoid infection. Speak to your optician for advice.

## Did you know?

You are born with <u>two sets</u> of teeth inside your mouth! The adult teeth that push out your baby teeth as you grow are present from birth, hidden deep inside your gums.

## Braces

If your teeth are a bit wonky or overcrowded, you might need braces. A special dentist called an **ORTHODONTIST** fits these, and you can have them for a few months or a few years, depending on how much your teeth need to move.

## Keeping your teeth squeaky <u>clean</u>

**BRUSH TWICE A DAY.** Every <u>morning</u> and <u>again</u> before bed.

**GENTLY BRUSH YOUR GUMS** with a circular motion when cleaning your teeth to keep gums strong. Scrub your tongue too to get rid of germs that make breath smell.

**FLOSS.** Remove all those bits of food and bacteria stuck between your teeth.

**VISIT YOUR DENTIST** twice a year. Yes, it's scary but you still have to go.

**AVOID FIZZY DRINKS,** your teeth hate the sugar. Also don't brush your teeth just after drinking fizzy pop or orange juice as this can wear away their hard protective coating.

There are <u>different types of braces</u> – some are clear and plastic, some are like metal bars, and some are brackets glued to the front of each tooth, with a wire running in between. You may feel self-conscious to begin with, but it'll all be worth it when you have lovely straight teeth!

# B.O. &
# PERSONAL HYGIENE

Sweat is a part of life. In fact, if we didn't sweat we'd be in real trouble, as perspiring (that's just a fancy word for 'sweating') is needed to cool our bodies down and stop them from overheating.

**TOGETHER WE MAKE A BEAUTIFUL STINK!**

## B.O.

Ready to learn about body odour? The first thing you need to know is that you have two types of **SWEAT GLANDS**. The first type work from the moment you're born, but the second type only start functioning during puberty – it sort of wakes them up, the lazy little things.

The second type of gland releases natural oils, which react with bacteria on your skin and cause body odour, also known as B.O. **POOOO-EY**.

**WHIFFY!**

Now that you have more sweat glands working (around three million in total!) you'll start to sweat more, especially your armpits. **B.O. CAN SMELL REALLY BAD**, so it's important to keep clean and fresh.

# Hygiene

Keep B.O. away by washing regularly. You should take a **SHOWER** at least every two days, and after every time you play sport, or just get very sweaty.

A quick rinse won't get rid of all that bacteria on your skin! Lather up some soap or shower gel and wash your body all over. You can also start using a gentle **DEODORANT** under your arms to kill the bacteria and stop the sweat smell.

## I have a question!

 **Should I wash inside my vagina as well as outside?**

No, please don't! Your vagina is very clever and is able to keep itself clean and healthy. Soaps can upset the delicate balance. But you can, and should, wash around your vulva (the outer area).

 **How can I make sure I don't smell?**

Deodorant is your biggest friend, as is washing your body and hair properly. Change your clothes regularly and wear clean underwear every day.

# ALL THINGS <u>FEET</u>

Feet are one of the first parts of your body to feel the effects of puberty, and can grow two or three sizes in a short space of time (so best hold off buying those really expensive shoes for a little while).

For girls, your feet usually reach full size about a year before you reach adult height and weight, so when they stop growing, you know you're nearly there. Also, because your body is not the same on both sides, one foot may be slightly larger than the other. Don't worry – this is **NORMAL!**

## Did you know?

The human foot contains a whopping 26 bones, 33 joints, 19 muscles and tendons, and 107 ligaments! That's a total of 52 bones per pair of feet!

## Ingrowing toenails

OUCH, OW and AAGH! Ingrown toenails happen when the corner or side of a toenail grows into the soft skin around it. It can be red, swollen and quite painful. It's important to treat these so that they don't get infected – if you think you have a pesky ingrown nail, go and see your doctor.

## What's that smell?

Just like the rest of your body, your feet have lots of sweat glands. This means that you need to wash them regularly to stop them getting **WHIFFY**. Beat the stink by wearing a nice, clean pair of socks or tights each day.

POO-EE!

## Best foot forward

High heels can cause problems for your feet and body. If you wear them all the time, you might develop **CORNS** (lumps of hard skin) and back or knee pain. It's best to wear <u>comfortable,</u> flatter shoes as much as you can, and only break out the heels for special occasions. Wearing flat shoes is just as cool!

## Verrucas

Verrucas are actually just ordinary <u>WARTS,</u> forced to grow inwards because they're on the soles of your feet. They can be painful but are easily treated with medicine from a chemist. They're also **VERY CONTAGIOUS**, and easily spread at swimming pools. Avoid this by wearing a special rubber swimming sock.

## Athlete's foot

Athlete's foot is a **FUNGAL INFECTION** that makes your feet all flaky and a bit gross! Fungus likes dark, damp and warm conditions – so make sure you change your sweaty socks as soon as you can. If you do get athlete's foot, it can be treated with an anti-fungal medicine.

# BOYS & PUBERTY

We've been talking about the changes girls go through as they grow up, but what happens to boys when the puberty train comes a'rolling into the station? **LET'S FIND OUT.**

**GOOD GRIEF!**

First up, boys usually start developing later than girls do – between the ages of 9 and 15. This means that for a year or two girls have a head start, and will often be taller (and more mature!) than a lot of the boys in their class. Explains a lot, doesn't it?

**JUST CALL ME MR MACHO!**

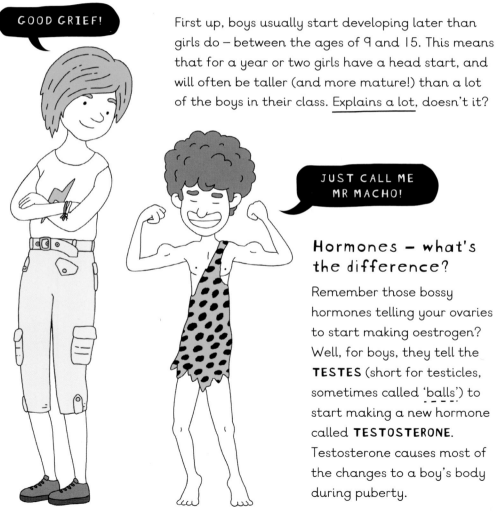

## Hormones – what's the difference?

Remember those bossy hormones telling your ovaries to start making oestrogen? Well, for boys, they tell the **TESTES** (short for testicles, sometimes called 'balls') to start making a new hormone called **TESTOSTERONE**. Testosterone causes most of the changes to a boy's body during puberty.

# The five stages of male puberty

**STAGE 1** New hormones are a **GO**. The testes start producing testosterone and **SPERM**, the male cell that creates a baby when it meets a female egg. Boys also start to get taller in this first stage, often shooting up suddenly, in what is known as a 'growth spurt'.

**STAGE 2** Boys' **TESTICLES** gradually grow larger, and hair begins to grow at the base of the penis. This is known as **PUBIC HAIR** because it grows near the pubic bone (part of the pelvis).

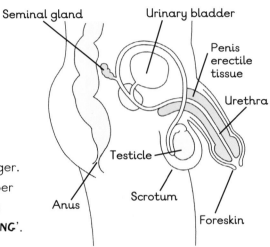

Seminal gland — Urinary bladder — Penis erectile tissue — Urethra — Testicle — Anus — Scrotum — Foreskin

**STAGE 3** The penis is growing longer. Boys' voices often start to get deeper at this stage too. This is sometimes referred to as their **VOICES 'BREAKING'**.

MUM, I THINK I MIGHT NEED TO START SHAVING!

**STAGE 4** Pubic hair continues to grow, and the penis gets thicker as well as longer. Skin starts to become oilier, which can cause **SPOTS** (see p.20). Hair also starts growing under the arms and on the upper lip and chin.

**STAGE 5** As puberty comes to an end, boys grow to their full adult height, and their shoulders get wider. **FACIAL HAIR** now grows regularly and many boys start shaving their faces.

31

# LOVE & RELATIONSHIPS

As puberty transforms you from girl to woman, it's normal for you to start having new and strong feelings of attraction towards others. **OOH LA LA!**

These feelings can make you want to be close to someone you're attracted to. You might feel all warm and tingly (**EEEEE!**) when you think about that person being your boyfriend or girlfriend, or get all tongue-tied when you see them (thanks for that, brain!).

**I THINK I'M IN LOVE!**

Sometimes liking someone in this way is called **'HAVING A CRUSH'** on them. Developing your first real crush is an exciting – and **SCARY** – time. You're dealing with unfamiliar emotions and there's a whole load of questions buzzing around your brain.

Do they like me too? Can people **TELL** that I like them? What should I do about these feelings?

## What to do with a crush

There are no set rules to follow – it's all about what you feel comfortable with. Talk to your friends about it if you like. These feelings are normal and natural; you don't have to hide them. If you want to tell the person you like that you fancy them, that's fine. If you don't, that's fine too. You're the boss!

## The science bit: hormones and L.O.V.E.

Most of the physical changes that happen during puberty are preparing your body to reproduce (have children) in the future. This means that your brain has to do the same – if you think boys are icky forever, there's not much chance you'll want to make a baby with one when you're grown up.

This is why the **HORMONES** that change your body also change your emotions. As you go through puberty, you'll start to develop romantic and, later, sexual feelings for other people. Just like everything else, this happens at different times for everyone.

## What is a relationship?

Having a boyfriend or girlfriend – a.k.a. being in a relationship – is a lot like friendship. You shouldn't feel pressured into doing anything you don't want to do, and should feel <u>happy</u> and <u>safe</u>, not scared or uncomfortable.

## Crushes: the good, the bad and the AAGH!

Having a crush can feel great... but bad too. If someone doesn't like you back, or breaks up with you, or is a famous celebrity you'll probably never meet (yes, Justin Bieber, we're looking at you), it feels **RUBBISH**.

Crushes can also feel like an obsession – you **CAN'T. STOP. THINKING.** about this person, and want to be near them **ALL. OF. THE. TIME.** These intense feelings might even seem as though they're taking over your life. **AAGH!**

### Did you know?

It's also fine to **NOT** like anyone in this way. Don't fancy anyone? No problem. There's no law that says you have to want a boyfriend or girlfriend. Trust us, we checked.

**I AM BROKEN - I WILL NEVER BE HAPPY AGAIN!**

Try to remember that you won't feel this way forever. You'll have lots of crushes in your lifetime, even if it seems as though this person is the only one for you right now. Sorry, Justin.

## I have a question!

 **I have feelings for another girl, not a boy – is this wrong?**

Of course not! How could such positive feelings ever be wrong? Being attracted to people the same sex as you is known as being gay and it's nothing to be ashamed of. Lots of people have same-sex crushes during puberty, and while some girls only ever fancy girls, others discover they like both boys **AND** girls.

 **How do I make my crush like me?**

You can't **MAKE** anyone like you. Be nice and friendly, and talk to them about your shared interests. Just be yourself! And remember: if they don't like you back, it might feel like the end of the world, but it's not. You **WILL** move on.

 **My friends are annoyed because I spend a lot of time with my boyfriend. What should I do?**

Life is all about balance. It's great that you like this boy and want to spend time with him, but don't forget your friends! Friendship is for life, so make time for them too.

35

# S.E.X. & HOW BABIES ARE MADE

When a man and a woman like each other, they have sexual intercourse, or 'sex' for short. When this happens a man's **PENIS** fills with blood and becomes hard – this is known as an 'erection'. He then inserts his erect penis into the woman's **VAGINA**.

## Sperm meets egg

During sex a man will ejaculate. This means that sperm comes out of his penis and into the woman's vagina. The sperm swim through the cervix and uterus, then head for the fallopian tubes. The first sperm to meet the egg **WINS THE RACE**, burrowing inside. The egg is now 'fertilized' and begins to tumble down the fallopian tube towards the uterus where it will embed itself into the wall of the womb.

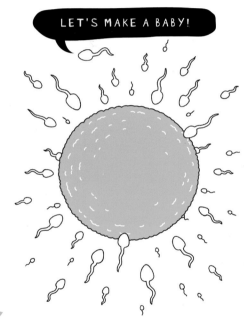

LET'S MAKE A BABY!

### REMEMBER

**NEVER** feel pressured into having sex because you're worried a boy won't like you if you don't, or because everyone else is doing it. It's a **HUGE** step that you should only take when you're ready.

Once a girl starts her periods, it means she's able to get pregnant. It's against the law to have sex before you're **16 YEARS OLD**, because it's a step you should only take when you're fully matured, and emotionally as well as physically ready.

# Girl parts: which bit is which?

**OVARIES:** Two egg-shaped sacs that contain millions of eggs. When an egg meets a sperm, they form an embryo, which will eventually grow into a baby.

**FALLOPIAN TUBES:** Eggs released from the ovaries travel down these tubes to the uterus.

**UTERUS (WOMB):** A fertilized egg attaches itself to the wall of the uterus. This is where the baby grows over the next nine months.

**VAGINA:** Your vagina is actually the bit **INSIDE** you, the canal that leads up to the lower part of your uterus, which is called the **CERVIX**.

**PUBIC HAIR:** The coarse, curly hair covering the pubic bone.

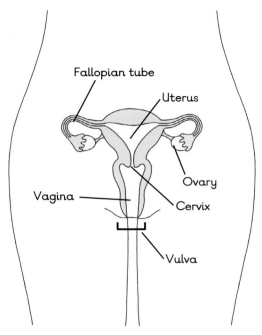

## Familiarize yourself

It's a good idea to become familiar with your most intimate parts. Try holding a hand mirror in between your legs to help you work out which bit is which.

**URETHRA:** A little hole above the opening to your vagina. This is connected to the bladder and is where your wee comes out.

**VULVA:** This is the **OUTER PART** of the vagina, which includes the outer lips (**LABIA MAJORA**) and inner lips (**LABIA MINORA**), as well as the clitoris (the teeny button right at the top).

**ANUS:** This is an opening in your bottom, connected to your stomach by your intestines. It's where poo comes out.

# CONTRACEPTION

Men and women have sex because they like it (yep, really), not just to make babies. This means they need to use a form of contraception. Contraception is also known as **'BIRTH CONTROL'** – it prevents a man's sperm from fertilizing a woman's egg, so that she doesn't become pregnant.

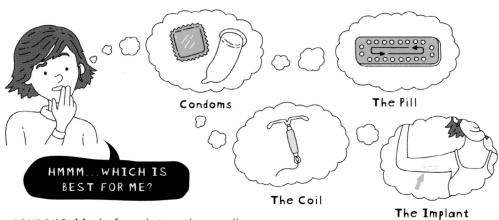

Condoms

The Pill

The Coil

The Implant

**HMMM...WHICH IS BEST FOR ME?**

**CONDOMS**: Made from latex, these roll onto a man's erect penis like a sort of one-fingered rubber glove. The space at the end catches sperm, stopping it from passing into the vagina. You can buy these, but you can also get them for free from places such as schools, chemists and health clinics.

**THE PILL**: The Pill is the common name for a hormone-based tablet that stops a woman's egg from attaching to the lining of her uterus. It must be taken every day to work.

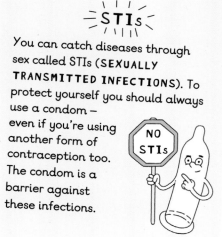

**STIs**

You can catch diseases through sex called STIs (**SEXUALLY TRANSMITTED INFECTIONS**). To protect yourself you should always use a condom – even if you're using another form of contraception too. The condom is a barrier against these infections.

NO STIs

**THE COIL**: This is a plastic or metal device that looks a bit like the letter 'T', and sits inside the uterus. It has to be fitted by a doctor but can be left in place for up to 10 years! It stops eggs from attaching to the lining of the uterus.

**THE IMPLANT**: Some women find remembering to take the pill annoying, so they choose to have the implant instead. This is about the size and shape of a hairgrip, and is placed just under the skin of the arm with a needle. It releases the same hormones used by the pill.

## I have a question!

 **Is it possible to get pregnant the first time you have sex?**

**YES, YES, YES!** You can become pregnant as soon as your ovaries start releasing eggs. This means that even if you haven't started your periods, you could still get pregnant, as the egg is released **BEFORE** the bleeding starts for the first time.

 **My boyfriend wants to have sex, but I don't. What should we do?**

You should only ever have sex when **YOU** are ready. Tell your boyfriend that you're not comfortable with taking that step yet. He should respect your decision. If he doesn't, then he's not worth your time.

 **What should I do if I think I'm pregnant?**

If you've had sex and think you might be pregnant, you should tell a trusted adult straightaway. It is a good idea to go to the doctor to talk about your options. Don't try and deal with it on your own or hope it will go away – it won't.

# HEALTHY EATING & FITNESS

Your body is the most precious thing you have, and *SPOILER ALERT*: you only get one, so it's important to look after it. Stay healthy as you grow and develop by eating a nutritious and balanced diet.

## REMEMBER

You should be eating three healthy meals a day: breakfast, lunch and dinner. Skipping meals isn't a good idea – your body works hard and it needs fuel to keep it going, just like a car.

## WHAT'S A BALANCED DIET?

Oh, we're so glad you asked. A balanced diet means eating a variety of foods containing the various vitamins and nutrients your body needs.

## Eat a lot of...

**FRUIT AND VEGETABLES**: Packed with goodness – you should eat at least five portions a day.

**CARBOHYDRATES**: Potatoes, pasta, rice, beans and brown bread keep your energy levels up.

**DAIRY**: Milk, cheese and yoghurt contain calcium, essential for keeping growing bones strong.

**PROTEIN**: Chicken, fish, soy, tofu, nuts and eggs are all packed with protein and are needed to maintain and build muscles you use every day.

BITE ME!

## Eat a little of...

**SUGARY FOODS:** Sweets, chocolate and fizzy drinks **SHOULDN'T** be part of your everyday diet!

**SALTY SNACKS:** Junk food and crisps have **LOADS** of salt, so save them for treats only. Too much salt can raise your blood pressure, which is bad for your heart, liver and kidneys.

## Eating disorders

An eating disorder is when someone develops an unhealthy and dangerous relationship with food. This may mean that they stop eating almost completely, which is a condition called **ANOREXIA**. Or they may make themselves sick – a condition known as **BULIMIA**.

Another eating disorder is **BODY DYSMORPHIA**. No matter how much weight a person loses, they still see themselves as 'fat'. Eating disorders lead to serious health problems and even death. If you have issues with food, **PLEASE** talk to someone who can help you.

## Exercise

Keeping **ACTIVE** is just as important as good food when it comes to staying healthy. Walking, running and playing sports are all great ways to exercise. You should do something that gets your heart pumping for at least <u>30 minutes a day</u>.

I'M A WINNER!

# BODY IMAGE

'Body image' is all about how you see yourself, and how you feel about yourself. Having a **HEALTHY, POSITIVE BODY IMAGE** means accepting who you are and feeling comfortable in your own skin.

## All shapes and sizes

When puberty starts, girls' bodies change in different ways. Some are curvy, some are petite, some are tall, some are short – but **ALL** are amazing. Having a positive body image is nothing to do with shape or size, and everything to do with how **YOU** feel about yourself. There is no 'perfect' or 'ideal' way a girl or woman should look. You are **BEAUTIFUL** whatever your body shape. Full stop.

Sometimes it can be hard to remember this when you're watching TV or flicking through a magazine, and all the females seem to be one kind of shape – but that's **NOT** real life.

42

# Get that positive body image feeling

**LOVE YOURSELF.** You are the only you there is, and that's a wonderful thing. Love the skin you're in and remember: life is about <u>being happy</u> and having fun, not about looking a certain way.

**DON'T COMPARE YOURSELF TO OTHERS.** This is the easiest way to end up feeling bad about yourself. OK yes, so you might wish you had hair like Harriet, or boobs like Bhavna, but they may be longing for a nose or eyes like Elesha – and that's not a good way to live!

**DON'T FORGET** that adverts on TV and in magazines sell things by making us feel dissatisfied with the way we look – that's their job. But we're all <u>unique</u> and beautiful in our own way, and our job is to enjoy life, so don't forget it!

**FOCUS ON THE GOOD.** If you're ever feeling bad about yourself, write down three **GOOD THINGS** you like about you. It could be your netball skills, your smile, your kindness – anything! The important thing is to be positive.

## REMEMBER

You don't love your friends and family because of the way they look, do you? You love them because of who they are on the inside – and the same goes for you. People will like you for your personality, not your body.

# BODY SHAMING

Body shaming is when someone makes <u>critical or negative</u> comments about the way someone looks, to their face or behind their back — and it's **NEVER OK**.

In fact, body shaming is a form of bullying, and sometimes people might not even realize they are doing it. Take a look at the following examples.

UGH LOOK AT THIS CELEBRITY, SHE'S SO FAT SINCE SHE HAD THAT BABY!

OH, DANIELLE, YOU'D BE SO MUCH PRETTIER IF YOU LOST SOME WEIGHT

LOOK AT PRIYA — SHE'S SO SKINNY, HER LEGS LOOK LIKE TWIGS!

GIRLS SHOULD HAVE LONG HAIR AND WEAR MAKE-UP; YOU'RE NOT A PROPER GIRL!

**WHICH DO YOU THINK SHOW BODY SHAMING?**

ANSWER: ALL OF THEM.

All of the girls or women mentioned above are being criticized about the way they look in some way. No, nope and **NOT OKAY**. Our differences are what make us human, and our <u>differences are great!</u>

## Lauren's story, age 13

### 'I WAS BODY SHAMED BY A FAMILY MEMBER'

'From about the age of nine, my aunt would always make mean comments about my weight. I think she thought she was just joking, but it made me feel terrible. Eventually my mum overheard her and went crazy – telling her I was a healthy size and shape for my age. She's stopped now – but I'll never forget how her words and comments made me feel. It has certainly made me careful not to make mean comments myself.'

## Beware of the media

Now that you know what body shaming is, you'll probably spot it in the media – that's newspapers, magazines, TV and films. Keep an eye out for anything that suggests there is a 'normal' or 'perfect' way for girls and women to look. When you see it, shout **BODY SHAMING** inside your head (or out loud, if you can), and remember that it's a load of nonsense.

Perfect Polly

# SOCIAL MEDIA & PHONES

Social media is the name for websites and apps that let you share pictures, videos and messages with your friends and family. **INSTAGRAM, SNAPCHAT, FACEBOOK, WHATSAPP** and **TWITTER** are all different types of social media. Easy, right? Whilst these are great fun to use, you must be very careful to use them safely and responsibly, as they can also be dangerous.

## REMEMBER

Life is like a jigsaw puzzle and social media is just a few pieces of that puzzle: it's not the whole picture.

## Staying safe online

**DO** keep your privacy settings **ON**, to make sure that only friends and family can see your posts.

**DO** block anyone who makes you uncomfortable or upset. A lot of apps have a 'report' button, so you can let them know if someone is being inappropriate or worrying.

**DO** remember that what you post on the internet is out there **FOREVER!** People can screenshot your pictures or comments, even if you delete them later.

## <u>Beware</u>...

**DON'T** have your full name as your username on sites like Instagram, Twitter, Snapchat etc.

**DON'T** add anyone that you don't know. They might be pretending to be someone they're not to get close to you. Besides, do you really want a stranger seeing all your pictures? **N-O-P-E**.

**DON'T** give **ANYONE** your personal details. This includes your address, where you go to school, your surname and your passwords.

**DON'T** post anything that might make someone feel sad or embarrassed. Put yourself in their position.

**DON'T** send pictures or messages you're not comfortable sending, and don't send anything to anyone you don't 100 per cent trust.

TELL ME ALL ABOUT YOURSELF

## Online life is **NOT** real life!

Social media can have a real effect on how we feel about ourselves. It might be that people from school are posting pictures from a party and you feel left out. Or perhaps all those celebs who seem to have perfect lives, skin and clothes are making your life seem a bit rubbish in comparison.

It happens to **ALL** of us, but here's what you need to remember: online life is **NOT REAL LIFE**. People only post what they want you to see on social media – pretty pictures don't show how someone is feeling inside.

# CYBERBULLYING

**SOCIAL MEDIA** is a great way for sharing and keeping in contact with your pals. But it has a dark side too, in the form of online bullying.

The problem with cyberbullying is that people can get to you constantly, at any time of the day, online. Whether you're chilling at home, or checking your phone on the bus, wherever you log in you are only fingertips away from abusive content. Not being able to escape from that is horrible, harmful and **NOT OK**.

Stupid!
So ugly.
Get a life.
Loser!

WHY ARE THEY BEING SO NASTY?

## Am I being cyberbullied?

You might not even realize that you are being cyberbullied, because you think what's happening to you is normal. It's not. Here's what to look out for:

1. Mean photos or comments about you.

2. Nasty or upsetting comments on your posts.

3. Being ganged up on.

4. Dreading going online.

## What to do

If you are being bullied in any way – online or otherwise – remember these four words: **DON`T SUFFER IN SILENCE.** You should never, ever, ever, think that nobody will listen to you, or believe you, or help you – there is **ALWAYS** someone you can talk to. Look at the handy list below.

WHAT'S WRONG?

WHY ARE THEY DOING THIS TO ME?

### Who can I talk to?

1. A parent or adult that you trust.

2. An older brother or sister.

3. A teacher.

4. A school counsellor or peer advisor.

5. A close friend.

Explain what's been going on and tell them how bad it's been making you feel. Save screengrabs of horrible comments or photos so that they can see for themselves. You could even keep a diary of events.

# BULLYING & PEER PRESSURE

Bullying comes in different forms and is when someone targets another person with repeated, deliberate, unpleasant behaviour. Some people who bully might use physical strength to **INTIMIDATE** others, but girls who bully are more likely to call the people they are targeting names, or exclude them from a friendship group.

Your school can help deal with this, so if you or anyone else are being bullied, **SPEAK UP** and tell a teacher what's going on. There are also anti-bullying websites that offer a safe space for advice and support.

TO BE MY FRIEND YOU MUST DRESS AND ACT LIKE ME!

YOU MAKE ME FEEL BAD ABOUT MYSELF

## What is a healthy friendship?

**A FRIENDSHIP SHOULDN'T:**

1. Make you feel bad about yourself.
2. Make you feel like you have to do or say things you don't want to.
3. Be hard work, or make you worry if you are liked.

**A FRIENDSHIP SHOULD:**

1. Be fun!
2. Be comfortable.
3. Be based on trust.

## What is peer pressure?

'**PEERS**' are people who are your age, like your classmates. If they try to persuade you to do something, or you feel like you have to act in a certain way to fit in, that's called 'peer pressure' – and **IT'S NOT OK.**

Always remember that it's **YOUR LIFE** and these are **YOUR DECISIONS** to make. If someone told you to put your hand in a fire, you wouldn't. So why would you let someone decide what happens to you in another way? **EXACTLY**.

HA! HA! HA!

### Peer pressure is...

**1.** Being encouraged to skip school. Bunking off won't just get you in trouble, but will also affect your learning, and your future – it's not worth it!

**2.** Being pressured to smoke cigarettes, drink alcohol or take drugs. All have a serious impact on your health. Whether or not you drink alcohol is a decision to make once you're over 18, but smoking and taking drugs – illegal or 'legal highs' – is ALWAYS really dangerous, and can lead to death. Just say NO.

**3.** Being forced to join in with bullying or leaving someone out. You might think that if you don't join in, you'll be left out next. This is a form of peer pressure.

**4.** Acting a certain way to fit in. Changing your normal behaviour so that you can join in and be 'cool' or popular is also peer pressure. Be yourself!

I BELIEVE IN ME!

# SCHOOL LIFE

School can be **HARD**, right? There are so many different lessons you want to do well in. You should always try your very best, but don't beat yourself up if you don't get top marks in everything.

Everyone is good at different things. Sarah might be a whizz at maths, but struggle in history. Lisa might be the best at art, but not so great at science. People have different strengths, and that is **A-OK**.

I WISH I WAS GOOD AT MATHS

## Dyslexia

Dyslexia is a learning condition that affects how the brain sees letters and symbols, making things like reading and telling the time difficult. Your school will support you if you're dyslexic. It's nothing to be embarrassed about and it doesn't mean you are any less intelligent than anyone else. In fact, dyslexics often have very **HIGH** intelligence. So there!

If you're struggling, **NEVER** be afraid to tell your teacher. If they know you're finding something difficult, they can help you. That is their job, after all!

## Too much pressure!

We've spoken about peer pressure, but parents can also put pressure on you, and that's difficult. Obviously you should <u>always</u> do your homework (even if it's a drag) but your life should have balance – there should be time for fun and relaxing after school too.

Feel like your **PARENTS** are expecting too much? Explain to them that you know they want you to be the best you can be, and that's what you want too! Make sure they realize that you're trying your hardest, and that you can't do more than that. Nobody – not even your parents! – should make you feel like you're not good enough.

MY BEST IS NEVER GOOD ENOUGH

## Girls and <u>STEM</u>

STEM is a short way of talking about **SCIENCE, TECHNOLOGY, ENGINEERING** and **MATHS**. There are lots of people trying to encourage more girls to enjoy and study these, and not be put off because they are seen as 'boy' subjects. This is great, because **a)** girls are awesome and there's no such thing as 'boy' or 'girl' subjects and **b)** because they lead to good jobs. If you like STEM, <u>stick with STEM</u>!

# SEXISM & GENDER EQUALITY

Men and women may have different types of bodies, but does that mean one is better then the other? **NO** – of course not! When people are treated unequally or are expected to act a certain way, just because they're a girl or a boy, it is called **SEXISM**.

## Give me an example!

**'Girls shouldn't play football – it's a boys' game!'** This is sexism. There is literally no reason why girls shouldn't play football, or any rule that says boys or girls have to like or do different things.

**'Matt's crying like a girl'** More sexism! It's totally normal for boys to cry if they're sad, and it doesn't make them any less male – that's an old-fashioned way of thinking.

I'M A FOOTBALL CHAMPION!

**'The woman should stay home to look after the children, and the man should go to work.'** Sound the sexism alarm! Men and women are equally capable, equally intelligent and equally able to work. There are lots of stay-at-home dads and working mums too. It's down to each individual to choose what they want to do.

## What is a feminist?

A feminist is anyone – male or female – who believes that men and women should be equal and treated exactly the same in all areas of life. That's it! Some people think feminism is about hating men, but that's not true. Everyone should be a feminist, because equality of rights and opportunity is important.

FIGHT FOR YOUR DREAMS!

### Girl power: a guide

1. Remind yourself every day that girls can do anything boys can do, and vice versa.

2. Don't let anyone tell you 'that's only for boys' – there's no such thing!

3. Look up to strong powerful women: Beyoncé, Malala Yousafzai, your mum... anyone who doesn't let men boss them around!

# FAMILY TALK

There are loads of different family types: single-parent, foster, step-families, two mums, two dads, or even being brought up by your grandparents, and no one type is better than another. What's important is that a family is **LOVING** and **SUPPORTIVE** – even if you do argue sometimes, or slam your door when you're in a mood.

## Marriage and divorce

When two people **LOVE** each other, they may decide to get married. But sometimes married people fall out of love and end the marriage, which is called 'getting a divorce'.

If your parents choose to get divorced, it can be very painful. It may seem like life as you know it is ending, and that can make you feel angry too.

### REMEMBER

If your parents are getting divorced, don't keep all those feelings inside of you – it'll only make you feel worse. Talk to your parents, they'll help you understand why this is happening.

The important thing to keep in mind is that it's **NOT YOUR FAULT**. Divorce is a personal thing between two people; there's nothing you could have done to prevent it. Sometimes adults just fall out of love with each other – it's very sad, but it happens. Your parents will always love **YOU**, no matter what. Divorce doesn't change that.

## Adoption

'Adoption' is when adults become the legal parents of a child they didn't give birth to. Being adopted isn't anything to be ashamed about – it makes you extra special because your parents **CHOSE** you. It also doesn't mean they are not really your parents: being a parent means supporting and loving a child as it grows. It doesn't matter if they made you or not.

## Step-families

One or both of your parents might choose to get married again, and their new wife or husband will be your step-mum or step-dad. If they already have children, these become step-brothers or step-sisters.

When two families come together, it is sometimes called a 'blended' family. It can be really great, but also difficult and strange. **ALWAYS** find someone to talk to about it all – don't try and muddle through on your own.

# DEPRESSION

There's a **LOT** to deal with when you're growing up, and this can make you feel down or upset from time to time. However, sometimes all the changes you're going through, or problems at home and school, can lead to a more serious condition called <u>depression</u>.

WHERE HAS THE SUNSHINE GONE?

## What is depression?

Depression is a <u>medical disorder</u>, and it's very different from just feeling a bit sad sometimes, or the mood swings that come with our good old friend puberty. People who are depressed find it almost impossible to stop feeling sad, for months or years at a time. It can make them feel worthless and unlovable, and they no longer enjoy the things they once did. They may spend a lot of time in bed, away from friends and family.

## How do I deal with it?

Unlike a sore throat or a broken arm, depression is a **MENTAL ILLNESS**, and there's no quick cure – you can't put a cast on someone's brain!

Doctors **CAN** treat depression, though, with medication and therapy. If you think you might be depressed, or feel like you want to hurt yourself, please, **PLEASE** speak to someone. Left untreated it will only get worse, so you **MUST** ask for help. We promise you – it **WILL** get better.

### Lara's story, age 13
**'I COULDN'T UNDERSTAND WHY I WAS ALWAYS SAD'**

'It happened slowly at first. I felt unhappy more and more often, and eventually didn't even want to do the things I used to love doing. It was like being trapped in a sad, grey bubble... all I wanted to do was lie in bed with the curtains closed, and I just couldn't stop crying. My mum was really worried so she took me to a doctor who diagnosed me with depression. Now I'm getting treatment, and seeing a therapist once a week to talk things through, and it's really helping.'

I HAVE A PROBLEM...

# GROWING UP <u>HAPPY</u>

Growing up isn't always easy. In fact, it can be the hardest time of your life. Your body and emotions change so quickly – in ways that are probably quite bewildering – that sometimes you struggle to keep up!

YIPPEE!

We hope that this book has given you some idea of what to expect from puberty and how to cope with everything that comes with it – and if there's one thing you should remember, it's this: **YOU CAN DO IT!**

## For support & advice*

**CHILDLINE:** 0800 1111
www.childline.org.uk

**NATIONAL BULLYING HELPLINE:**
07734 701 221
www.nationalbullyinghelpline.co.uk

**THE SAMARITANS:** 116 123
www.samaritans.org

**SWITCHBOARD LGBT+ HELPLINE:**
0300 330 0630
www.switchboard.lgbt

## Who can help?

The best piece of advice we can give you is never go it alone. If you're struggling, **TALK TO SOMEONE.** That can be a trusted adult, a friend or a trained professional. Here are some websites and helplines that can help:

\* CHILDREN SHOULD BE SUPERVISED WHEN USING THE INTERNET, PARTICULARLY WHEN USING AN UNFAMILIAR WEBSITE FOR THE FIRST TIME. THE PUBLISHERS AND AUTHOR CANNOT BE RESPONSIBLE FOR THE CONTENT OF THE WEBSITES REFERRED TO IN THIS BOOK.

# Positive puberty

**REMEMBER** that you're not the first person to have felt this way, or to have gone through puberty. Every single adult you see dealt with the P-word and came out the other side, so **YOU CAN TOO!**

**SAY** 'I am **STRONG** and powerful and I can deal with anything' three times, out loud. Yes, you might feel a bit silly, but it actually works.

**DO SOMETHING** that makes you howl with **LAUGHTER** – whether it's watching your favourite TV programme, being silly with a friend, or tickling your little sister until she squeals!

**WRITE DOWN** three things you like about yourself, however small. If you're feeling sad or down, look at this list and remember why you are **SPECIAL**.

**REMEMBER** that **EVERYONE** is different, and that's what makes the world go round. Difference is good, difference makes us human.

**CONFIDENCE** is key. We don't mean being loud, or the centre of attention – but having confidence in yourself, and who you are. Love yourself, and the world will too.

You are a strong, **BRILLIANT** and amazing human being, taking your first steps down the road to adulthood and the rest of your life. That's exciting, and even if there are a few bumps and hurdles along the way, just keep walking down that road – you **WILL** get through it all.

# GLOSSARY

**ANOREXIA NERVOSA** A serious illness / eating disorder characterized by an obsessive desire to lose weight and extreme dieting.

**ANUS** The hole in your bottom that solid waste (poo) passes through when you go to the toilet.

**BODY IMAGE** How you see yourself – being aware of what your body looks like.

**BODY SHAMING** Making critical or negative comments about someone based on their size or weight, or what they look like.

**BULIMIA NERVOSA** A serious illness / eating disorder characterized by intentionally vomiting food shortly after eating.

**BULLYING** The repetitive, intentional hurting of one person or group by another person or group, where the relationship involves an imbalance of power.

**CERVIX** The entrance to the uterus at the top of the vagina.

**CLITORIS** A sensitive bump, just above the hole that your wee comes out of. When gently touched, it creates a nice feeling that can lead to orgasm.

**CONTRACEPTION** Methods for preventing pregnancy during sexual intercourse.

**DISCHARGE** Any fluid passed out of the human body – from the vagina in particular.

**FALLOPIAN TUBES** The tubes leading from the ovaries to the uterus.

**FOLLICLES** Tiny holes in your skin from which hairs grow.

**GLAND** A cell or organ that makes chemical substances and then releases them into the body.

**HORMONE** A chemical substance made by glands and then transported around the body.

**OESTROGEN** A hormone, mainly produced by the ovaries, that develops the female body.

**OVARIES** The female reproductive organs which produce eggs.

**OVULATION** The release of eggs from a woman's ovaries.

**PITUITARY GLAND** A pea-sized gland at the base of the brain that releases hormones.

**PUBERTY** The process which takes place when a girl's body gradually changes to become a woman (and a boy's body changes to become a man).

**PUBIC BONE** A protective bone at the front of the pelvis.

**PUBIC HAIR** Hair growing near your vagina and covering your pubic bone.

**SANITARY TOWEL** An absorbent pad that sticks to your underwear to soak up blood during a period.

**TAMPON** A small, tightly packed wad of cotton wool, which is inserted into the vagina to absorb blood during a period.

**VAGINA** The tube that leads from the cervix to an outer opening, in between the urethra and anus. It is very stretchy so a baby can come out.

**VERRUCAS** Small painful warts on the soles of your feet.

**VULVA** The outside parts that cover and protect the opening to the vagina. This includes outer and inner lips, the urethra and the clitoris.

**URETHRA** A tiny tube that takes urine (wee) from the bladder to the outside of your body. The end of the urethra forms a small opening in your body just above the opening to the vagina.

**UTERUS** A hollow organ within the abdomen of a woman, in which a baby grows. Also known as a 'womb'.

# INDEX

# A GUIDE FOR GROWN-UPS

Puberty doesn't just affect those going through it – it can also be a **CHALLENGING** and daunting time for families and teachers. This book is designed to help not only girls making the transformation from child to adult, but also you.

It can be a great idea to read this book together. For you, it can act as a guide on how to discuss the physical and emotional changes that come with puberty. For a child, it allows time to ask **QUESTIONS** about puberty and all that comes with it.

If your daughter or pupil would rather read this book alone, suggest having a chat after she's finished, to answer any questions she might have.

Let her know that she can **TALK** to you whenever she needs to. Sometimes all you need to do is listen; at other times she might need **ADVICE** from someone who's been through all this before. Either way, knowing she has your support is invaluable.

Men also have an important role in influencing a young girl's health, well-being and the way in which she comes to view the opposite sex. Be confident in your approach to the content in this book, **TEACHING** her that talking openly and never being embarrassed to ask for advice or help is the foundation of growing up happy.

**TEACHERS** are incredibly important, too. Check that your school policy, which should be developed in consultation with parents and pupils, supports you when teaching and answering questions. If you feel it needs updating or amending, set the wheels in motion and make this happen!

## Lead the way

Young girls look to us to set an example of strong, confident **WOMANHOOD**. How we act and behave affects their perception of the world, so love the skin you're in, and be a positive role model for the next generation!

LET'S LOOK AT THIS TOGETHER